Vicki J. Kuyper

EVERYDAY

Praise

*An Infusion of
Spiritual Wisdom from
the Psalms*

Spiritual Refreshment
for Women

BARBOUR
PUBLISHING

© 2010 by Barbour Publishing, Inc.

Writing and compilation by Vicki J. Kuyper in association with Snapdragon Group^SM, Tulsa, Oklahoma, USA.

ISBN 978-1-60260-958-7

Cover design: Kirk DouPonce, DogEared Design

Published by Barbour Publishing, Inc., P.O. Box 719, Uhrichsville, Ohio 44683, www.barbourbooks.com

Our mission is to publish and distribute inspirational products offering exceptional value and biblical encouragement to the masses.

ecpa Member of the
Evangelical Christian
Publishers Association

Printed in India.

Contents

Trust in the LORD and do good.
Then you will live safely
in the land and prosper.
Take delight in the LORD,
and he will give you
your heart's desires.
Commit everything
you do to the LORD.
Trust him, and he will help you.

PSALM 37:3–5 NLT

Introduction

As women, we can learn a lot about passion, emotion, and praise through the poetry of the book of Psalms. There were at least six authors—perhaps more—and they were nothing if not real. They cried out to God unabashed, and their prayers seem to put our own struggles into words: *Where is God when I hurt? How can I forgive? Can I be forgiven? Are You really listening, God? Can I depend on You?*

Whether you're looking for an uplifting way to begin your day or seeking what the Bible has to say about a specific topic that's relevant to your life, *Everyday Praise* is designed to help you draw near to the God who offers help, hope, and healing.

Abundance

All sunshine and sovereign is GOD,
generous in gifts and glory.
PSALM 84:11 MSG

You have a Father who owns the cattle on a thousand hills and holds the cosmos in His hands. This Almighty Father generously offers all He has to you. He offers you a life overflowing with joy, comfort, and blessing. But like any gift, this one has to be accepted before it can be enjoyed. Today, why not say yes to the Father who loves you? Tell Him how you long to live—and love—like His cherished child.

> I have God's more-than-enough,
> more joy in one ordinary day
> than they get in all their
> shopping sprees.
>
> PSALM 4:7 MSG

An "abundant life" is not something we
can pick up at the mall or purchase online.
It comes from recognizing how much we
receive from God each and every day.
While some of our abundance may come
in the form of possessions, the overflow
of an abundant life ultimately comes
from what fills our hearts, not our closets.
Resting in God's "more-than-enough" can
transform a desire to acquire into a prayer
of thanksgiving for what we've already been
given.

Acceptance

The LORD has heard my cry for mercy;
the LORD accepts my prayer.

PSALM 6:9 NIV

People talk about "accepting" God into their lives. But it's God's acceptance of us that makes this possible. Because Jesus gave His life to pay the price for all the wrongs we've ever done, our perfect God can accept us wholeheartedly, even though we're far from perfect people. God not only accepts us, He also accepts our imperfect prayers. We don't have to worry about saying just the right words. The "perfect" prayer is simply sharing what's on our hearts.

I hate all this silly religion, but you,
GOD, I trust. I'm leaping and singing
in the circle of your love.

PSALM 31:6 MSG

Religion is man-made, not God-made.
Having a personal relationship with God is
something totally different. It's not a list of
rules and regulations or something we only
"do" on Sundays. It's a love story between
Father and child, a relationship in which
we're totally accepted and unconditionally
loved. Since we can't earn God's acceptance—
it's a free gift of grace—that means we can't
lose it either. God's acceptance releases us
from the fear of rejection, so we're free to
truly be ourselves.

Accomplishment

You give me your shield of victory,
and your right hand sustains me;
you stoop down to make me great.

PSALM 18:35 NIV

Accomplishing something worthwhile
is one of the joys of living. It can give
you a sense of purpose and worth. But
you are more than the sum of your
accomplishments. You are an accomplished
woman simply by continuing to mature into
the individual God created you to be. Enjoy
using every gift, talent, and ability God has
so generously woven into you while resting
in the fact that you are worthy of God's
love, regardless of what you've
achieved.

> Unless the LORD builds
> the house, its builders
> labor in vain.
>
> PSALM 127:1 NIV

We were designed to do great things hand in hand with a very great God. So why not invite God to be your coworker in every endeavor you undertake today? Call on Him throughout the day, anytime you need wisdom, peace, or perseverance. Allow God to infuse you with creativity, humility, and compassion, regardless of the size of the task at hand. Your hard work, guided by prayer and undergirded by the Spirit of a mighty God, can accomplish amazing things.

Appearance

I praise you because I am fearfully
and wonderfully made.

PSALM 139:14 NIV

You are a living, breathing reason for
praise. God formed only one of you, unique
in appearance, intricate in design, priceless
beyond measure. You were fashioned with
both love and forethought. When you look
in the mirror, is this what you reflect upon?
If not, it's time to retrain your brain. Use the
mirror as a touchstone to praise. Ask God,
"What do You see when You look at me?"

Listen quietly as God's truth helps retool
your self-image.

With your very own hands you
formed me; now breathe your wisdom
over me so I can understand you.

PSALM 119:73 MSG

God isn't concerned with appearances.
The Bible tells us God looks at peoples'
hearts instead of what's on the outside.
Perhaps that's because appearances can
be deceiving. A woman can be beautiful in
the world's eyes, while her heart nurtures
pride, deceit, lust, greed, or a host of other
unlovely traits. By learning to look at people
the way God does, from the inside out,
we may discover beauty in others—and in
ourselves—that we've never noticed before.

Assurance

The LORD will work out his plans for
my life—for your faithful love,
O LORD, endures forever.

PSALM 138:8 NLT

Throughout scripture, God continually
reassures us that He's working on our
behalf to accomplish the good things He has
planned for our lives. If your confidence
wavers, if you need to know for certain
someone is on your side, if you're anxious
about the future, do what people who've felt
the very same way have done for centuries:
Take God's words to heart. There's no
greater assurance than knowing you're
loved, completely and eternally.

> The LORD will watch over your
> coming and going both now
> and forevermore.
>
> PSALM 121:8 NIV

Conventional wisdom tells us that nothing lasts forever. Thankfully, just because a saying is often quoted doesn't make it true. The time-tested wisdom of the Bible assures us that God always has been and always will be. Because of Jesus, *forever* is a word that can apply to us as well. When we follow Jesus here on earth, we follow Him straight to heaven. We have the assurance of knowing our true life span is "forevermore."

Attitude

What kind of day will you have today?
Your answer might be, "I won't know until
I've lived it!" But the attitude with which
you approach each new day can change
the way you experience life. That's why
it's important to set aside some "attitude
adjustment time" every morning. When you
wake, remind yourself, "This is the day the
Lord has made." Look for His hand in the
details and thank Him for every blessing
He brings your way.

The Lord is my strength
and my shield; my heart trusts in him,
and I am helped.

PSALM 28:7 NIV

A rock, a fortress, a warrior, a king—the Bible uses many metaphors to describe God. Since no single word can wholly describe our infinite, incomparable God, word pictures help us better connect a God we cannot see with images that we can. If your attitude could use a boost of strength and confidence, picture God as your shield. He is always there to protect you, to shelter you, and to guard your heart and mind.

Belief

You have always been God—long
before the birth of the mountains,
even before you created
the earth and the world.

PSALM 90:2 CEV

People once believed the world was flat.
This meant only the most intrepid explorers
would venture long distances and risk
falling off the "edge" of the earth. What
people believe determines the choices they
make, no matter what era they live in. What
do you believe about God? Does it line up
with what the Bible says? It's worth checking
out. Since you will live what you believe,
it's important to be certain what you
believe is true.

> I would have lost heart, unless
> I had believed that I would see
> the goodness of the Lord in the
> land of the living.
>
> PSALM 27:13 NKJV

Knowing a friend's heart toward you can help you relax and be yourself. With a friend like this, you can honestly share your deepest secrets, feelings, and failures without fear of ridicule or reprisal. The psalms remind us over and over again that God's heart toward us is good. Believing in God's innate goodness means we can entrust every detail of our lives to Him without hesitation.

Bible

You thrill to GOD's Word,
you chew on Scripture day and night.

PSALM 1:2 MSG

Imagine God's words as your favorite meal, each bite a delicacy to be savored and enjoyed. You relish the unique blend of ingredients, the flavor and texture. When the meal is complete, you're nourished and satisfied. Scripture is a well-balanced meal for your heart and soul, a meal that can continue long after your Bible is back on the shelf. Ponder what you've read. Meditate on God's promises. Chew on the timeless truths that add zest to your life.

Every word you give me is a miracle
word—how could I help but obey?
Break open your words,
let the light shine out, let ordinary
people see the meaning.

PSALM 119:129 MSG

The Bible isn't a novel to be read for entertainment, a textbook to be skimmed for knowledge, a manual for living, or a collection of inspirational sayings. The Bible is a love letter. It's the story of God's love for His children from the beginning of the world until the end—and beyond. It's a book that takes time to know well, but God promises His own Spirit will help us understand what we read. All we need to do is ask.

Blessings

I said to myself, "Relax and rest.
GOD has showered you
with blessings."

PSALM 116:7 MSG

Friends know what friends need," so the
saying goes. That's one reason why friends
often throw baby showers for moms-to-be.
It's a way to help provide what a mom will
need in the months to come. God knows
us, and our needs, better than any friend or
family member. That's why He throws us a
shower every day. God wraps His blessings
in wisdom, purpose, and creativity to help
meet our physical, emotional, and
spiritual needs.

> May God be gracious to us and
> bless us and make his
> face shine upon us.

PSALM 67:1 NIV

When people speak of "blessings," they're often referring to words. Blessings are given at meals and weddings. "Bless you" is even said after a sneeze. The words we say can be as much of a gift as the blessings we can hold in our hands. What would God have you say to the people you meet today? Consider how you can bless others with your words—then speak up. A good word can often be the perfect gift.

Burdens

Cast your burden on the LORD, and
He shall sustain you; He shall never
permit the righteous to be moved.

PSALM 55:22 NKJV

Casting a fishing line is an almost
effortless motion. Casting a burden paints
a totally different image. Burdens are
pictured as heavy, cumbersome, not easily
carried—let alone "cast." But casting our
burdens on God is as easy as speaking to
Him in prayer. It's calling for help when we
need it, admitting our sin when we've fallen,
and letting our tears speak for our hearts
when words fail us.

Praise be to the Lord,
to God our Savior,
who daily bears our burdens.

PSALM 68:19 NIV

Some things are too heavy to carry alone. A couch, for instance. Or a washing machine. The same is true for the mental and emotional burdens we bear. The good news is that strength, peace, comfort, hope, and a host of other helping hands are only a prayer away. We're never alone in our pain or struggle. God is always near, right beside us, ready to help carry what's weighing us down.

Challenge

Our Lord is great, with limitless
strength; we'll never comprehend
what he knows and does. GOD puts
the fallen on their feet again.

PSALM 147:5–6 MSG

During a track and field event, it isn't
uncommon to see an athlete trip over one
of the hurdles and tumble to the ground.
What brings the crowd to its feet is when
the runner gets back up. Challenge involves
risk, in sports and in life. Don't be afraid of
trying difficult things. Whether you succeed
or fail, God promises to renew your strength
and purpose. You may not understand how,
but you can be certain He's able.

> The LORD is near to all
> who call on him, to all
> who call on him in truth.
>
> PSALM 145:18 NIV

Some mornings you wake up with the knowledge that a challenging day is ahead of you. Other times, difficulty catches you by surprise. Whatever challenge enters your life, remind yourself that the Lord is near. Not only will God help you meet each challenge head-on, but He will use each one to help you grow. Look for God's hand at work in your life, helping you achieve what may seem impossible.

Change

But what the LORD has planned
will stand forever.
His thoughts never change.

PSALM 33:11 CEV

Our God isn't wishy-washy. He doesn't experience bad hair days or mood swings, nor is He swayed by trends, fads, or peer pressure. Our perfect, eternal God has no peer. From scripture we can tell that God experiences emotions like love, grief, and pleasure. However, He isn't driven by His emotions, as we sometimes are.

That means we can trust God to be true to His promises, His plans, and His character—today, tomorrow, and always.

I trust in you, O LORD; I say,
"You are my God."
My times are in your hands.

PSALM 31:14–15 NIV

Change can be exciting. It can also be
uncomfortable, unwanted, and at times
even terrifying. If you're facing change and
find yourself feeling anxious or confused,
turn to the God of order and peace. He
holds every twist and turn of your life in His
hands. Try looking at change through God's
eyes, as an opportunity for growth and an
invitation to trust Him with your deepest
hopes and fears.

Character

Test my thoughts and find out
what I am like.

PSALM 26:2 CEV

Some women spend a great amount of
time trying to look beautiful on the outside,
while paying little attention to what's on
the inside. God's words and His Spirit can
help reveal the true you, from the inside out.
Ask God where your character needs some
touching up—or perhaps a total makeover.
See if your thoughts, your words, and your
actions line up with the woman you'd like
to see smiling back at you in the mirror
each morning.

> Only you can say
> that I am innocent, because
> only your eyes can see
> the truth.
>
> PSALM 17:2 CEV

Not everyone will understand the unseen story behind what you say and do. There will be times when you're misunderstood, slandered, or even rejected. This is when your true character shines through. How you respond to adversity and unfair accusations says a lot about you and the God you serve. Ask God to help you address any blind spots you may have about your own character. Treat your critics with respect. Then move ahead with both confidence and humility.

Children

Then our sons in their youth
will be like well-nurtured plants,
and our daughters will be like pillars
carved to adorn a palace.

PSALM 144:12 NIV

Good food, a good night's sleep, a good
education, a good home that's safe and
overflowing with love. . . Good mothers try
to provide what their children need. But
children need more. Like adults, children
have spiritual needs as well as physical and
emotional ones. That's why praying for your
children every day is more than just a good
idea. It's a reminder that your children
need more than motherly love. They
also need their heavenly Father's
involvement in their lives.

Sons are a heritage from the LORD,
children a reward from him.

PSALM 127:3 NIV

A child is a gift that is literally heaven-
sent. You don't have to have children of
your own to care about the kids around
you—or to learn from them. In the New
Testament, Jesus talks about how our
faith should resemble that of a child's.
To understand why, consider this:
Children believe what they hear, love
unconditionally, and say what they think.
What a wonderful way to relate to God.

Choices

My choice is you, GOD, first and only.
And now I find I'm your choice!

PSALM 16:5 MSG

Some choices we make change the course
of our lives, such as whether we'll remain
single or marry, what career we'll pursue,
whether or not to adopt a child. But there's
one choice that changes not only the
direction of our lives, but our eternity.
When we choose to follow God, it affects
every choice we make from that moment
forward. The more we involve God in our
decision process, the wiser our choices
will be.

> Guide my steps by your word,
> so I will not be
> overcome by evil.
>
> PSALM 119:133 NLT

When you're driving along an unfamiliar highway, road signs are invaluable. They point you in the proper direction and warn you of impending danger. When it comes to the road of life, the Bible is a sign that helps guide you every step of the way. The more you read it, the better prepared you are to make good choices. When facing a fork in the road of life, stop to consider which direction God's Word would have you go.

Comfort

GOD's a safe-house for the battered,
a sanctuary during bad times.
The moment you arrive, you relax;
you're never sorry you knocked.

PSALM 9:9–10 MSG

When women are in need of comfort, they seem to instinctively turn to a spouse or close friend. There's nothing wrong with seeking a human shoulder to cry on when you need it. Just remember that the Bible refers to Jesus as both our bridegroom and friend. The comfort God provides runs deeper than anything people can offer.

God sees your problems as part of a larger, eternal picture and can offer perspective as well as solace.

The LORD is close to the
brokenhearted and saves those
who are crushed in spirit.

PSALM 34:18 NIV

Putting your faith in Jesus doesn't mean
you'll never have a broken heart. Scripture
tells us even Jesus wept. Jesus knew the
future. He knew His heavenly Father was in
control. He knew victory was certain. But
He still grieved. When your heart is broken,
only God has the power to make it whole
again. It won't happen overnight. But when
you draw close to God, you draw close to the
true source of peace, joy, and healing.

Commitment

He always stands by his
covenant—the commitment he
made to a thousand generations.

PSALM 105:8 NLT

God has made a commitment to you
similar to a wedding vow. He promises to
love and cherish you through sickness and
health, prosperity or poverty, good times
and bad. But with God, this commitment
doesn't last until "death do you part." Even
in death and beyond, God is there. There's
nothing you can do that will make Him turn
His face from you. His commitment to love
and forgive you stands steadfast, come
what may.

*I will never give up hope or
stop praising you.*
PSALM 71:14 CEV

Choosing to follow God is not a one-
time commitment. It's a choice that's
made anew each day. Who, or what, will you
choose to follow today? Culture or popular
opinion? Your emotions or desires? Or
God and His Word? Staying consistently
committed to anything—a diet, an exercise
program, a spouse, or God—takes effort.
But with God, His own Spirit strengthens
us and gives us hope to help us remain fully
committed to Him.

Compassion

As a father has compassion on
his children, so the Lord has
compassion on those who fear him.

PSALM 103:13 NIV

If your children are hurting, you don't
think twice about coming to their aid. You
listen attentively to their heartaches, dry
their tears, and offer them words of wisdom
and encouragement. As God's child, you
have a perfect and powerful heavenly
Father who feels this way about you. His
compassion is more than emotion. It's love
in action. You can tell God anything,
without fear of condemnation or
abandonment. God's forgiveness runs
as deep as His love.

But you, O Lord, are a
compassionate and gracious God,
slow to anger, abounding in love
and faithfulness.

PSALM 86:15 NIV

Without love and compassion, an all-
powerful God would be something to fear
instead of Someone to trust. That's one
reason why Jesus came to earth: to help us
see the compassionate side of the Almighty.
Throughout the Gospels, we read how Jesus
reached out to the hurting—the outcasts, the
infirm, the poor, and the abandoned. He
didn't turn his back on sinners, but embraced
them with open arms. His arms are still open.
Will you run toward His embrace?

Confidence

My heart is confident in you,
O God; my heart is confident.
No wonder I can sing your praises!

PSALM 57:7 NLT

In the Bible, when a word or phrase is
repeated, it's time to pay attention. In the
original language of the Old Testament,
this signifies that something is the best,
the ultimate, the *pièce de résistance*! The
psalmist in Psalm 57 doubly notes how
confident his heart is in God. No wonder
praise comes naturally to him! Take it
from the psalmist: You need never doubt
God's heart toward you. You can be
confident—eternally confident—
in Him.

> Those who are righteous
> will be long remembered.
> They do not fear bad news;
> they confidently trust the LORD
> to care for them. They are
> confident and fearless and can
> face their foes triumphantly.

PSALM 112:6–8 NLT

We live in uncertain times, economically, politically, and globally. Yet you can greet each new day with your head held high, confident and unafraid. Why? Because you have a God who cares deeply about you and the world around you. When your confidence is placed firmly in God instead of your own abilities, bank account, or "good karma," you need not fear the future. It's in God's powerful, capable, and compassionate hands.

Contentment

The LORD is my shepherd,
I shall not be in want.

PSALM 23:1 NIV

When it comes to brains, sheep are not the sharpest crayons in the box. They frighten easily, tend to follow the crowd, and have limited abilities for defending themselves. That's why sheep thrive best with a shepherd who guides, protects, and cares for their needs. Our Good Shepherd will do the same for us. Worry, fear, and discontent are products of a sheepish mentality.

However, the peace of true contentment can be ours when we follow God's lead.

I've cultivated a quiet heart.
Like a baby content in its mother's
arms, my soul is a baby content.

PSALM 131:2 MSG

Picture a well-fed newborn resting in her mother's arms, peacefully gazing up into her eyes. That's contentment. No worrying about "Does this diaper make me look fat?" No fears over "Will social security be around when I retire?" No burning desire for a nicer stroller or a bigger crib. Allow God to baby you. Gaze into His eyes by recalling the ways He's provided for you. Cultivate contentment by trusting Him as a mother is trusted by her child.

Courage

*When I called, you answered me;
you made me bold and stouthearted.*

PSALM 138:3 NIV

Women are often characterized as timid
creatures—fleeing from spiders, screaming
over mice, cowering behind big, burly
men when danger is near. But the Bible
characterizes women of God as bold and
courageous. Queen Esther risked her life to
save God's children from genocide. Deborah
led an army and judged the tribes of Israel.
Rahab dared to hide Jewish spies to save her
family. Today God will supply the courage
you need to accomplish whatever He's
asked you to do.

> Wait on the LORD;
> Be of good courage, and He
> shall strengthen your heart;
> Wait, I say, on the LORD!
>
> PSALM 27:14 NKJV

Foolhardiness can look like courage at first glance. However, true courage counts the cost before it forges ahead. If you're faced with a risky decision, it's not only wise to think before you act, it's biblical. Ecclesiastes 3:1 (MSG) reminds us, "There's an opportune time to do things, a right time for everything on the earth." Waiting for that right time takes patience and courage. Don't simply pray for courage. Pray for the wisdom to discern that "opportune time."

Daily Walk

Clean the slate, God, so we can
start the day fresh! Keep me
from stupid sins, from thinking
I can take over your work.

PSALM 19:13 MSG

Yesterday is over. Today is a brand-new day.
Any mistakes or bad choices you've made
in the past are behind you. God doesn't
hold them against you. He's wiped your past
clean with the power of forgiveness. The
only thing left for you to do with the past
is learn from it. Celebrate each new day by
giving thanks to God for what He's done and
actively anticipating what He's going to
do with the clean slate of today.

Scheduling time to pray and read the Bible can feel like just another item on your to-do list. But getting to know God is not a project. It's a relationship. Best friends don't spend time together just because they feel they should. They do it because they enjoy each other's company and long to know each other better. The more consistent you are in spending time with God each day, the closer "friend" you'll feel He is to you.

Decisions

I say to GOD, "Be my Lord!"
Without you, nothing makes sense.

PSALM 16:2 MSG

Paper or plastic. Right or left. Yes or no.
Every day is filled with decisions that need
to be made. Some have little bearing on the
big picture of our lives, while others can
change its course in dramatic ways. Inviting
God into our decision-making process is
not only wise, but helps us find peace with
the decisions we make. Knowing God is at
work, weaving all our decisions into a life
of purpose, helps us move forward with
confidence.

GOD is fair and just;
He corrects the misdirected,
sends them in the
right direction.

PSALM 25:8 MSG

When you're driving in an unfamiliar city, a map is an invaluable tool. It can help prevent you from taking wrong turns. If you do wind up headed in the wrong direction, a map can help set you back on track. God's Word and His Spirit are like a GPS for your life. Staying in close contact with God through prayer will help you navigate the best route to take in this life, one decision at a time.

Desires

All my longings lie open before you,
O Lord; my sighing is not
hidden from you.

PSALM 38:9 NIV

What does your heart long for most? Talk
to God about it. He'll help you uncover the
true root of your deepest desires. Longing
for a child? Perhaps what you're really
longing for is unconditional love. Longing
for a home of your own? Perhaps it's your
need for security or to be admired by others
that you crave. Ultimately, God is the only
one who can fill your deepest longings—
and it's His desire to do exactly that.

> Delight yourself in the LORD
> and he will give you the
> desires of your heart.
>
> PSALM 37:4 NIV

To "delight" in someone is to take great pleasure from simply being in that person's presence. If you truly delight in God, the deepest desire of your heart will be to draw ever closer to Him. This is a desire God Himself delights in filling. That's because God delights in you. You are more than His creation. You are His beloved child. He delights in you like a proud father watching his daughter take her very first steps.

Devotion

I will walk in freedom,
for I have devoted myself
to your commandments.

PSALM 119:45 NLT

Being devoted to someone you love is one thing. Being devoted to doing something, like completing a project or following God's commandments, is quite another. It doesn't sound as passionate or pleasurable, but devoting yourself to do what God asks isn't a self-improvement program. It's a labor of love. Commitment is a way of expressing love, whether it's honoring your marriage vows or devoting yourself to doing what's right. Love is a verb, always in action, making invisible emotions visible.

Protect me,
for I am devoted to you.
Save me, for I serve you
and trust you. You are my God.

PSALM 86:2 NLT

The heart of devotion isn't duty. It's love. The deeper your love, the deeper your devotion. What does being devoted to God look like? It's characterized by a "God first," instead of "me first," mentality. While it's true that being devoted to God means you'll spend time with Him, it also means you'll give your time to others. Your love of God will spill over onto the lives of those around you. Your devotion to God is beneficial to everyone!

Encouragement

The humble will see their God at
work and be glad. Let all who seek
God's help be encouraged.

PSALM 69:32 NLT

There's encouragement in answered
prayer. Sometimes God's answers look
exactly like what we were hoping for. Other
times they reveal that God's love, wisdom,
and creativity far surpass ours. To be aware
of God's answers to prayer, we have to keep
our eyes and hearts open. Be on the alert
for answers to prayer today. When you
catch sight of one, thank God. Allow the
assurance of God's everlasting care to
encourage your soul.

As soon as I pray, you answer me;
you encourage me by
giving me strength.

PSALM 138:3 NLT

A word of encouragement can go a long way in strengthening our hearts. Whether that word comes from a friend, a spouse, a stranger, or straight from God's own Word, encouragement has power. It lets us know we're not alone. We have a support group cheering us on as we go through life. Out of that support group, God is our biggest fan. He wants you to succeed, and His help is just a prayer away.

Endurance

Those who trust in the LORD
are like Mount Zion, which cannot
be shaken but endures forever.

PSALM 125:1 NIV

Alpine peaks endure sun and showers,
heat and hail. They don't yield or bow to
adverse conditions, but continue to stand
firm, being exactly what God created them
to be—majestic mountains. God created you
to be a strong, victorious woman. You were
designed to endure the changing seasons of
this life with God's help. Lean on Him when
the winds of life begin to blow. God and His
Word are solid ground that will never
shift beneath your feet.

Invigorate my soul so
I can praise you well, use your
decrees to put iron in my soul.

PSALM 119:175 MSG

A marathon runner doesn't start out running twenty-six miles. She has to start slow, remain consistent, and push herself a bit farther day by day. That's how endurance is built. The same is true in life. If what lies ahead seems overwhelming, don't panic thinking you need to tackle everything at once. Ask God to help you do what you can today. Then celebrate the progress you've made, rest, and repeat. Endurance only grows one day at a time.

Eternal Life

I'll bless you every day,
and keep it up from now to eternity.

PSALM 145:2 MSG

Eternal life isn't a reward we can earn.
It's a free gift given by a Father who wants
to spend eternity with the children He
loves. This gift may be free to us, but it was
purchased at a high price. Jesus purchased
our lives at the cost of His own. His death on
the cross is the bridge that leads us from this
life into the next. Forever isn't long to say
thank you for a gift like that.

You will show me the way of life,
granting me the joy of your
presence and the pleasures of
living with you forever.

PSALM 16:11 NLT

Johann Wolfgang von Goethe wrote, "Life is the childhood of our immortality." In light of eternity, you're just a kid—regardless of your age. In today's youth-obsessed society, keeping your "true" age in mind can help you see each day from a more heavenly perspective. Hold on to your sense of childlike wonder. Allow it to inspire awe, thanks, praise, and delight. Draw near to your heavenly Father and celebrate. There's so much more to your life than meets the eye.

Example

I will study your teachings
and follow your footsteps.
PSALM 119:15 CEV

In the Bible we read about heroes like
Abraham, Moses, and David. Though these
men did admirable things, they were also
flawed. They made mistakes and poor
choices. Nevertheless, God used them in
remarkable ways. The only person in the
Bible who lived a perfect life was Jesus. He is
our ultimate example. If you're searching for
the best way to live and love, Jesus' footsteps
are the only ones wholly worth following.

My life is an example to many,
because you have been my
strength and protection.

PSALM 71:7 NLT

If people follow your example, where
will it lead? Will they find themselves
headed toward God or away from Him?
As you allow God to change you from the
inside out, your life will naturally point
others in His direction. Being an example
worth following doesn't mean you're under
pressure to be perfect. It's God's power
shining through the lives of imperfect
people that whispers most eloquently,
"There's more going on here than
meets the eye. God is at work."

Expectations

Trusting God can help transform you into a "glass half full" kind of person. You can face every day, even the tough ones, with confidence and expectation because you're aware there's more to this life than can be seen. You can rest in the promise that God is working all things together for your good. You know death is not the end. In other words, you can expect that great things lie ahead. Why not anticipate them with thanks and praise?

> The eyes of all look expectantly to You, and You give them their food in due season.
>
> PSALM 145:15 NKJV

Praying without expecting God to answer is kind of like wishing on a star. You don't believe it's going to make any difference, but you do it anyway—just in case there really is something behind all those fairy tales. When you pray, do so with great expectations. God is at work on behalf of a child He dearly loves—you. Just remember, God's answers may arrive in ways and at a time that you least expect.

Faith

The LORD protects those
of childlike faith.

PSALM 116:6 NLT

Feel like you need more faith? Sometimes
what we really need is the courage to act on
what we already believe. A skydiver may
have faith her parachute is packed correctly,
but that doesn't stop her stomach from
doing its own loop-de-loop as she jumps out
of the plane. However, the more she dives,
the less nervous she feels. The better you
know God, the more a leap of faith feels like
a hop into a loving Father's waiting arms.

Lead me by your truth
and teach me, for you are the
God who saves me. All day long
I put my hope in you.

PSALM 25:5 NLT

Faith is both a gift we receive and an
action we take. God's Spirit gives us enough
faith to reach out to a Father we cannot see.
But as we continue reaching—continue
putting our trust in God as we go through
life—that little gift of faith grows stronger,
like a muscle consistently put to work at
the gym. Give your faith a workout today by
doing what you believe God wants you
to do.

Faithfulness

The LORD is good. His unfailing love
continues forever, and his faithfulness
continues to each generation.

PSALM 100:5 NLT

With time, we come to believe certain
things are unshakable. The sun rises and
sets. The tides ebb and flow. Seasons revolve
year after year. Babies are born, people
die, and the world goes on pretty much as it
has for centuries: faithful to a predictable
pattern. But there will come a time when
the world as we know it will end. Only God
is totally unshakable and unchanging.

His love and goodness to us will remain
forever faithful.

The LORD is faithful to all
his promises and loving
toward all he has made.

PSALM 145:13 NIV

There's an old saying that warns,
"Promises are made to be broken." With
God, the opposite is true. The Bible is filled
with promises God has made and kept. With
a track record like that, it means you can
trust God's Word and His love for you. He
remains faithful, even if your faithfulness
to Him wavers from time to time. God
and His promises have stood the test of
time and will remain steadfast throughout
eternity.

Family

God sets the lonely in families.

PSALM 68:6 NIV

Family can be one of our greatest joys in this life. It can also be messy, because it's where we show our true colors. It's where we're real. That's why "family" is the perfect petri dish for us to learn how to love like Jesus. Unconditional love sees others for who they really are, warts and all, and continues to reach out, sacrifice, and forgive. As we allow God to love us, He will help us more readily love others.

*O God; you have given me
the heritage of those
who fear your name.*

PSALM 61:5 NIV

Your true lineage extends far beyond
the branches on your family tree. That's
because you have a spiritual heritage as well
as a physical one. Your family line extends
back through Old and New Testament
times, around the world, and right up into
today. You may know some of your brothers
and sisters by name. Others you may not
meet until you walk the streets of heaven
together. But God's children are family,
linked by faith and a forever future.

Feelings

Look at him; give him
your warmest smile.
Never hide your feelings from him.

PSALM 34:5 MSG

People often ask "How you are?" as a
formality. What they want to hear is "Fine!"
Nothing more. But God wants more than a
passing acquaintance with you. He invites
you to share not only what you want and
need, but also how you feel. God created you
as a woman with complex emotions. You
need never hesitate to share your tears, or
even a hormonal outburst, with the One
who knows you and loves you through
and through.

When doubts filled my mind,
your comfort gave me renewed
hope and cheer.

PSALM 94:19 NLT

What are your emotions telling you today? You're unloved? Insignificant? A failure? Powerless to change? What you feel is not always an accurate measure of what is real. When your emotions try to take you on a roller-coaster ride, refuse to buckle yourself in. Ask God to help you sort through what's going on in your mind and heart. Cling to what God says is true, not to what your fickle emotions whisper on a poor self-image day.

Fellowship

I will praise you in the
presence of your saints.

PSALM 52:9 NIV

Fellowship is a fancy word for getting together with others who love God. It's more than going to church. It's doing life together. Whether you're meeting as a small group for Bible study or simply chatting one-on-one over a cup of coffee about what God is doing in your lives, you're experiencing fellowship. When faith and friendship come together with honesty and authenticity, relationships thrive—between you and God and between you and your spiritual brothers and sisters.

> I will give you thanks in the
> great assembly; among throngs
> of people I will praise you.

PSALM 35:18 NIV

There's beauty and power in drawing close to God each morning to talk to Him about the day ahead. But you are just one of God's children. Sometimes it's great to get the family together for prayer and worship. Every Sunday, in churches around the world, that's exactly what's happening. God's family is getting together for a Thanksgiving celebration. Like any family get-together, your presence adds to the joy. So join in! God's church wouldn't be the same without you.

Finances

If your wealth increases,
don't make it the center of your life.

PSALM 62:10 NLT

Money is an important tool. You can use it to repair your car, pay your rent, or help put food on the table. But it's just a tool. Loving it would be like loving a socket wrench. It can't love you back or change who you are. It can only do its job. Ultimately, the true value of a tool depends on how well you use it. Allow God to show you how to wield your finances wisely.

Do not be overawed when a man
grows rich, when the splendor
of his house increases.

PSALM 49:16 NIV

It's been said that "money talks."
Sometimes it yells. Loudly. The things it
buys helps draw attention to those who have
it and to those who would do anything to
get it. But money says absolutely nothing
about who a person really is—or how
rich he or she truly is. You have riches
that exceed what's in your bank account.
Every relationship you invest in, be it with
God, family, or friends, is a treasure that
increases in value over time.

Forgiveness

You are forgiving and good,
O Lord, abounding in love
to all who call to you.

PSALM 86:5 NIV

The fact that God is perfect can be
intimidating, especially when you consider
that God knows everything you've ever
done. But our perfect God is also perfectly
forgiving. There is nothing you can do, or
have done, that will make Him turn away
from you. When you ask for forgiveness,
you have it. No groveling. No begging. All
you need do is come to Him in humility and
truth. Jesus has taken care of the rest.

> As far as the east is from the
> west, so far has he removed
> our transgressions from us.
>
> PSALM 103:12 NIV

Picture a chalkboard. Written on it is everything you've ever done that goes against what God has asked of you. What would you see written there? How big would the chalkboard be? Now imagine God wiping it clean with one swipe of His hand. Nothing remains, not the faintest image of one single word. That's how completely God has forgiven you. When guilt or shame over past mistakes threatens to creep back into your life, remember the empty chalkboard—and rejoice.

Freedom

> But let me run loose and free,
> celebrating GOD's great work, every
> bone in my body laughing, singing,
> "God, there's no one like you."
>
> PSALM 35:9 MSG

Knowing you're loved without condition sets you free. It invites you to abandon insecurity, relax, and enjoy being yourself. It encourages you to go ahead and try, because failure is simply a steep learning curve. God's acceptance of you is the key to this freedom. As you rest in God's absolute acceptance, you'll discover the confidence and courage you need to push beyond who you are today and become the woman you were created to be.

I run in the path of your commands,
for you have set my heart free.

PSALM 119:32 NIV

Suppose there were no traffic laws. Going out for a drive would be a dangerous endeavor. Drivers would have to fight their way down the road. Traffic would be a snarled mess. Following rules can sound like the opposite of freedom. But without rules, community turns into chaos. Following God's commands protects us from harm and helps us love God and others well. It frees us to travel the road of life unencumbered by fear, uncertainty, or insecurity.

Friendship

And these God-chosen lives
all around—what splendid
friends they make!

PSALM 16:3 MSG

Thank God for friendship. Literally.
Spending time with those who understand
how you tick, remind you what a wonderful
woman you are, and challenge you to reach
your God-given potential is one of life's
greatest joys. The best way to have great
friends is to be one. Pray regularly for the
women God brings into your life, asking
God to help you love them in ways that help
you grow closer to each other and to Him.

*How wonderful, how beautiful,
when brothers and
sisters get along!*

PSALM 133:1 MSG

The feel of sandpaper rubbing against unfinished wood isn't pleasant. Neither is the experience of two good friends rubbing each other the wrong way. But when friends are authentic and vulnerable with each other, it's bound to happen—and that's a good thing. It helps bring our weaknesses to light. Helping smooth out one another's rough edges is part of God's plan. If friendship hits a rough patch, stay close and work through the friction. Let love help you grow.

Fruitfulness

*Your wife shall be like a fruitful vine
in the very heart of your house,
your children like olive plants
all around your table.*

PSALM 128:3 NKJV

There are many ways to be fruitful. One
way is through relationships. Whether it's
with family, friends, neighbors, church
members, or coworkers, the things you
say and do can be buds that blossom into
something beautiful. Who will you spend
time with today? Each encounter is an
opportunity to plant a seed. Will it be a seed
of encouragement, grace, faith, comfort,
or. . . ? Ask God to help you know the
type of seed others need.

And may the Lord our God show
us his approval and make our
efforts successful. Yes, make
our efforts successful!

PSALM 90:17 NLT

If you plant an apple tree, you probably
hope to enjoy its fruit someday. But hoping,
and even praying, won't guarantee a good
harvest. A fruit tree needs to be watered,
pruned, and protected from bugs, frost,
and hail. It needs God's gift of life *and* your
loving care. The same is true for any project
you're working on. Work hard, pray hard,
and wait patiently for God's good timing.
Then, when harvesttime arrives, remember
to give thanks.

Future

All the days ordained for me
were written in your book before
one of them came to be.

PSALM 139:16 NIV

The story of your life is written one day at a time. Every choice you make influences the chapters yet to come. But one thing is certain—the ending. Your future was written the moment you chose to follow God. That means the end of your story here on earth is actually a brand-new beginning. It's a story with endless chapters, a "happy eternally after" where tears are history and true love never fails.

You make my life pleasant,
and my future is bright.

PSALM 16:6 CEV

It's been said that we don't know what the future holds, but we know who holds the future. Tomorrow is not a potluck of chance possibilities. The Bible tells us that God is at work, bringing something good out of every situation His children face. Knowing a God who deeply loves us and is in control, no matter what comes our way, allows us to hold our heads high and walk toward the future with confident expectation.

Generosity

Good will come to him who
is generous and lends freely,
who conducts his affairs with justice.

PSALM 112:5 NIV

A funny thing happens when you get in the habit of sharing what God has given you. The more you give, the more you realize how blessed you are and the more grateful you become—which inspires you to share even more of what you have with others. It's a wonderful cycle that loosens your grip on material things so both your hands and your heart can more freely reach out to those around you.

An evil person borrows and never pays back; a good person is generous and never stops giving.

PSALM 37:21 CEV

Love and generosity are two sides of the same coin. Both put the needs of others before their own. Both give without expecting anything in return. Both make our invisible God more visible to a world in need. As our love for those around us grows, generosity can't help but follow suit. Today take time to become more aware of the needs of those around you. Then ask God to help you act on what you see with loving generosity.

Gentleness

You are my God. Show me what you
want me to do, and let your gentle
Spirit lead me in the right path.

PSALM 143:10 CEV

God doesn't drag His children through life
by the wrist like a domineering parent with
a self-centered agenda. God leads with love,
gently and quietly. God's Spirit whispers,
"Go this way," as a verse of scripture crosses
your mind. He tenderly nudges your
conscience toward making good choices and
reaching out in love. He brings comfort in
countless creative ways that those who don't
recognize Him label as coincidence.

God's gentleness reminds us that His
power is always tempered by love.

> You have also given me the
> shield of Your salvation;
> Your right hand has held me up,
> Your gentleness has
> made me great.

PSALM 18:35 NKJV

A children's fable describes the sun and wind making a bet: Who can get a man to take off his coat? The wind blows with vengeance, using his strength to try and force the man's hand. The sun simply shines, gently inviting the man to shed what he no longer needs. God does the same with us. His gentleness warms us toward love and faith. The closer we draw to God, the more we'll treat others as He's treated us.

Goodness

Worship GOD if you want the best;
worship opens doors
to all his goodness.

PSALM 34:9 MSG

In the Old Testament book of Exodus we
read about Moses, a man God referred to
as "friend." When Moses asks to see God's
glory, God shows Moses His goodness.
Afterward, Moses' face literally glows.
When we worship God, we glimpse His
goodness. We focus on who He is, what
He's done, and what He's promised is yet
to come. Our faces may not glow like
Moses', but glimpsing God's goodness
is bound to bathe our hearts in joy.

"Only you are my Lord!
Every good thing I have is
a gift from you."

PSALM 16:2 CEV

What is good about your life? Consider how every good thing we receive can be tied back to God. Family. Friends. Talents. The ability to earn an income. It's easy to take the good things in our lives for granted, while readily putting the blame on God when we feel things go wrong. The next time you notice you're feeling happy about something good in your life, look for the part God played in sending it your way.

Grace

For the LORD God is our sun and our
shield. He gives us grace and glory.
The LORD will withhold no good thing
from those who do what is right.

PSALM 84:11 NLT

When a gift is wrapped in grace, it comes
with no strings attached. That's the kind
of gift God gives. He doesn't hold eternal
life just out of reach, taunting, "If you try
harder, this can be yours." He doesn't
promise to love us if we never mess up
again. He doesn't say He'll forgive, but
refuse to forget. God graces us with gifts we
don't deserve, because His love is deeper
than our hearts and minds can
comprehend.

> GOD is good to one and all;
> everything he does is
> suffused with grace.
>
> PSALM 145:9 MSG

If a driver in front of you unexpectedly pays your toll, you can't help but feel in her debt. It's a kindness you didn't deserve and can't repay. Jesus' death on the cross was more than a random act of kindness. It was part of an eternal plan. It was also a gift of grace. Jesus paid a high toll for your sins. You can't repay Him. All you can do is gratefully accept what He's given.

Guidance

The LORD says, "I will guide you along the best pathway for your life. I will advise you and watch over you."

PSALM 32:8 NLT

If you're on safari, a knowledgeable guide will lead you to the best vantage point to see wildlife, educate you on what you're seeing, and protect you from danger. God is like a safari guide who never leaves your side. He knows both the joys and the dangers that surround you. Through His Spirit and scripture, God will guide you toward a life of wonder and adventure. Stay close to His side and allow Him to lead.

I praise you, LORD, for being my guide. Even in the darkest night, your teachings fill my mind.

PSALM 16:7 CEV

Suppose you learn CPR in a first-aid class. Years later, when a child nearly drowns at a neighborhood pool, you spring into action. You know exactly what to do. The same is true with the Bible. The better acquainted you become with God's words, the more readily they come to mind when you need them most. When you're unsure of which way to turn, turn to the Bible. It will help lead you where you ultimately want to go.

Happiness

Live a happy life!
Keep your eyes open for GOD,
watch for his works; be alert
for signs of his presence.

PSALM 105:3–4 MSG

Babies often smile when they catch sight of their mother's face. Catching a glimpse of God can do the same for us. It can make our hearts happy. Yet God's presence is much more subtle than that of a human parent. God reveals Himself in quiet ways, such as in an answer to prayer, the glory of a sunset, or the gift of a new friend. Keep your eyes open. God is ever present and at work in your life.

> You have helped me,
> and I sing happy songs
> in the shadow of your wings.
>
> PSALM 63:7 CEV

Happiness can be contagious. Why
not spread some of yours around?
Consider the ways God helps you nurture
a happy heart. How has He comforted you,
encouraged you, strengthened you? If you're
happy, share it. Tell someone close to you
what God has done. Smile warmly at those
who cross your path. Surprise someone with
a gift just because. Express to God how
you feel in song. Thank God for the little
things—such as the ability to feel happy.

Health

Your body is amazingly resilient, yet terminally fragile. Fashioned by God's lovingly creative hand, it was not designed to last. But you were. That's because you are so much more than your body. But God cares about all of you, your body and your soul. Even if your health fails, He will not. He is near. He hears every prayer, even those you hesitate to pray. Call on Him. His hope and healing reach beyond this life into the next.

He renews our hopes
and heals our bodies.
PSALM 147:3 CEV

Good health is a matter of both prayer and practice. As with every detail of our lives, God wants us to share our health concerns with Him. But God also asks us to take an active role in caring for our bodies. The way we care for a gift reveals what we truly feel about the giver, as well as what we've received. Practicing healthy habits is a thank-you note to God for His gift of life.

Help

Do something, LORD God,
and use your powerful arm
to help those in need.

PSALM 10:12 CEV

God spoke the cosmos into being. He fashioned the ebb and flow of the tides. He breathed life into what was once nothing more than dust. This same awesome God is reaching down to offer His help to you today. Perhaps your prayer is for your own needs. Or maybe it's for those you care about but don't know how to help. God is mighty enough, and loving enough, to do the impossible.

> You listen to the longings
> of those who suffer.
> You offer them hope,
> and you pay attention
> to their cries for help.
>
> PSALM 10:17 CEV

*H*elp! is a prayer every heart knows
how to pray, even those who are unsure if
there's a God who's listening. It's a cry that
acknowledges that life is out of our control—
and a deep-seated hope that Someone is
ultimately in charge. Our desperate cries do
not disappear into thin air. God hears every
prayer, sees every tear, and doesn't hesitate
to act. God's answers and timing are
not always what we expect, but they
are what we need.

Honesty

Open up before GOD,
keep nothing back; he'll do
whatever needs to be done.

PSALM 37:5 MSG

You can't keep a secret from God. He knows you inside and out. That doesn't mean you can't hold out on Him. There may be things you'd rather not discuss: areas of shame, bitterness, or rebellion. He'll never muscle His way into those parts of your heart. He's waiting for an invitation. If you're honest about wanting real change in your life, don't wait any longer. Open up before God. Grace, forgiveness, and healing are yours for the asking.

Think of the bright future waiting
for all the families of honest and
innocent and peace-loving people.

PSALM 37:37 CEV

Honesty is more than just telling the truth. It's living it. When you conform to the expectations of those around you instead of focusing on maturing into the individual God designed you to be, you rob the world of something priceless—the unique gift of you. You also rob yourself of the joy and freedom that come from fulfilling your God-given potential. When it comes to being the true you, honesty truly is the best policy.

Hope

Happy is he who has the God
of Jacob for his help,
Whose hope is in the LORD his God.

PSALM 146:5 NKJV

Some people place their hope in financial security. Others hope their popularity, abilities, or connections will get them where they want to go. Still others hope that if they want something badly enough, it'll just happen. But only those who place their hope in God can face tomorrow without any fear of the future. When you trust in God, you do more than hope for the best. You rest in knowing God's best is His plan for your life.

> The LORD is there to rescue
> all who are discouraged and
> have given up hope.
>
> PSALM 34:18 CEV

It's easy to lose heart when your focus is on difficulties that persist day after day. That's why reconnecting with God every morning is so important. Time together reminds you that an all-knowing and all-powerful God is in your corner, ready and able to help. It helps you sift the trivial from the eternal. And it restores hope to its rightful place in your life, where it can shine a light on God's goodness and faithfulness to you.

Humility

Though the LORD is great, he cares
for the humble, but he keeps
his distance from the proud.

PSALM 138:6 NLT

Beloved child, rebellious daughter;
faithful friend, self-centered competitor;
fully forgiven, fickle and flawed; priceless
miracle, nothing but dust: You are the
sum of all of these things and more.
Acknowledging that you're a crazy quilt
of weakness and strength is a step toward
humility. After all, true humility isn't
regarding yourself as less significant
than others. It's seeing yourself the way
God does, as no more or less than you
truly are.

In your majesty, ride out to victory,
defending truth, humility,
and justice. Go forth to perform
awe-inspiring deeds!

PSALM 45:4 NLT

Remembering that only God is God keeps us humble. Sounds simple enough. But all too often we try to grab the wheel from God's hands and steer our lives in the direction of what looks like it will make us happy instead of simply doing what God asks us to do. Invite God to expose any areas of your life where pride has you heading in the wrong direction. Ask Him to reveal to you how big He really is.

Integrity

Joyful are people of integrity,
who follow the instructions
of the LORD.

PSALM 119:1 NLT

Modern culture tells us that "bad girls" have all the fun. Don't believe it. A self-centered life is an empty life. When you choose to follow God and live a life of integrity, regret no longer knocks at your door. In its place you find joy. There are no worries about your past catching up with you or some half-truth being exposed. You're ready to live life to the fullest, a life in which love and respect are freely given and received.

> I will lead a life of integrity
> in my own home.
>
> PSALM 101:2 NLT

Chameleons may be interesting to watch on the nature channel, but they're not something worth emulating in terms of character. Consistency in the way we live our lives—whether we're on the job, at home with family, or out on the town with friends—is a hallmark of integrity. If how we act is dependent on who we're with, we may be seeking the approval of others more than seeking God. In terms of integrity, whose approval are you seeking today?

Joy

Where morning dawns and evening
fades you call forth songs of joy.

PSALM 65:8 NIV

Happiness is usually the result of circumstance. Joy, however, bubbles up unbidden, often persisting in spite of circumstance. It's an excitement that simmers below the surface, an assurance that God is working behind the scenes, a contentment that deepens as you discover your place in the world. The more at home you feel with God, the more joy will make a home in your heart—a welcome reminder that God is near.

You turned my wailing into
dancing; you removed my sackcloth
and clothed me with joy.

PSALM 30:11 NIV

Some seasons of life pull you into the
shadows. But God wants to help you make
your way back into the light—not because
you shouldn't mourn, but because every
season heralds a new beginning. There is
joy ahead, even if you can't see it or feel
it right now. Each day brings you closer
to those first flutters of joy. Watch for
them. Wait for them. Pray for them. Then
celebrate their arrival with thanks and
praise.

Justice

Words of wisdom come when good
people speak for justice.

PSALM 37:30 CEV

It takes courage to stand up for what's right,
especially if you're the only voice speaking
up in the crowd. But words have power. They
can help bring injustice to light. They can
encourage others to take a stand. They can
incite change. But the right motive is just
as important as the right words. Ephesians
4:15 tells us to speak "the truth in love."
Truth tempered with love is the perfect
agent of change.

For all who are mistreated,
the LORD brings justice.

PSALM 103:6 CEV

If watching the evening news leaves
you feeling that life isn't fair, take it as
a sign that you've inherited your heavenly
Father's sense of justice. The way people
are treated in this world is not always fair or
loving. Sometimes they're used, abused, and
then tossed aside. But with God, justice will
prevail. God knows each person's story and
will make things right in His perfect time
and in His wise and loving ways.

Kindness

Kindness turns criticism into encouragement, bad news into words of comfort, and discipline into teachable moments. That's because kindness is concerned with more than results. It's also concerned with people's hearts. God's plan for you is bigger than being a "good person." God also wants you to be healed and whole. You can trust God to be a loving Father and not a callous taskmaster, because the breadth of His kindness stems from the depth of His love.

With all my heart
I praise the LORD! I will never
forget how kind he has been.

PSALM 103:2 CEV

Kindness is a quiet side of love. It isn't showy, demanding center stage. It often serves in the background meeting needs, offering a word of encouragement or an impromptu hug. Sometimes kindness even travels under the name "anonymous." Likewise, the kindnesses God showers upon our lives often fall into the anonymous category. They're the coincidences, the unexpected pleasures, the little things that lift our hearts during a difficult day. How has God's kindness enriched your life this week?

Leadership

You guided your people like
a flock of sheep, and you chose
Moses and Aaron to be their leaders.

PSALM 77:20 CEV

Think of the leaders in your life. The
list may include a boss, pastor, Bible
study leader, mentor, chairperson, or the
government officials helping steer the
direction of the country you live in. The
Bible encourages us to support and pray
for our leaders. It doesn't add a disclaimer,
saying this applies only if we like them,
agree with them, or voted for them. How
would God have you pray for your
leaders today?

> Don't put your life in the
> hands of experts who know
> nothing of life, of salvation life.
>
> PSALM 146:3 MSG

Those we choose to follow have power over us. Their influence can affect our actions, as well as our way of thinking. They can help draw us closer or steer us farther away from God. But sometimes we're not even aware of whom we're letting lead. Celebrities, experts in various fields, the media, charismatic friends—whose footsteps are you following? Ask God to help you discern who besides Him is worthy to lead the way for you.

Learning

I will instruct you and teach
you in the way you should go;
I will counsel you and watch over you.

PSALM 32:8 NIV

To learn, you have to listen. Are you really listening to what God is trying to teach you? Whether it's reading the Bible, listening to a message at church, or receiving counsel from someone who is farther down the road of faith than you happen to be, there is always more to learn. Prepare your heart with prayer. Ask God to help you clearly understand what you need to learn and then act on what you hear.

*The godly offer good counsel;
they teach right from wrong.*

PSALM 37:30 NLT

Want to run a marathon? Talk to those who've run one before. They know how to train, which shoes to buy, and what to expect when the big day arrives. The same is true if you want to go the distance with God. When you meet people who have followed God for many years, ask questions. Discover what they've learned, where they've struggled, and how they study the Bible. You may gain new friends, as well as godly counsel.

Life

Teach us to use wisely
all the time we have.

PSALM 90:12 CEV

Want to live life in a way that honors God?
There are so many options it's hard to know
what to do. But in Matthew 22:37–39, Jesus
sums up the purpose of life by saying we're
to love God and love others. Prayerfully
weighing the choices before us against
these two commands can help us make wise
decisions. We don't know how long our
lives will be, but with love as our goal, we're
certain to use our time well.

Who out there has
a lust for life?
Can't wait for each day
to come upon beauty?

PSALM 34:12 MSG

God is amazingly creative and incomparably loving. Having Someone like that design a plan for your life is an exciting prospect. God promises there are good things ahead for you. That promise is enough to make each morning feel like a chest filled with treasure just waiting to be opened. Greet each new day with expectation. Invite God to join you in your search for the extraordinary treasures He's scattered throughout even the most ordinary of days.

Loneliness

I am lonely and troubled.
Show that you care
and have pity on me.

PSALM 25:16 CEV

In Genesis we read about creation. God declared everything He created "good," with one exception. God said it was not good for Adam to be alone. God designed people to be in relationships with each other and with Him. When you're feeling lonely, God agrees: It's not good. Ask God to bring a new friend your way and help you connect more deeply with those already in your life. But for right now, invite God to meet your deepest need.

PSALM 59:17 MSG

When you're feeling lonely, picture God beside you in the room. Talk to Him the way you would a dear friend. If praying aloud feels awkward, journal or write God a love note that you can tuck in your Bible. Read the book of Psalms. See what other people had to say to God when they felt the way you do right now. Remember, God is with you, whether you're aware of His presence or not.

Love

As high as the heavens are above the earth, so great is his love for those who fear him.

PSALM 103:11 NIV

It's hard to grasp how deeply God cares for us, because our firsthand experience of love comes from relationships with imperfect people. But God's love is different. With God, we need never fear condemnation, misunderstanding, or rejection. He completely understands what we say and how we feel—and loves us without condition. Since God is never fickle or self-centered, we can risk opening up every part of our lives to Him. We can risk returning the love He so freely gives.

> I am like an olive tree growing in God's house, and I can count on his love forever and ever.
>
> PSALM 52:8 CEV

How do you love someone you can't see, hear, or touch? The same way you love an unborn child. You learn everything you can about what that child is like. You speak to it, even though it doesn't speak back. When you finally meet face-to-face, you find you're already in love. Yes, you can love someone you cannot yet see. As for God, His love for you transcends eternity. You're the child He's loved since before there was time.

Mercy

Surely goodness and mercy
shall follow me all the days of my life;
and I will dwell in the house
of the LORD forever.

PSALM 23:6 NKJV

In old-fashioned melodramas and
classic films, repentant scoundrels throw
themselves on the mercy of the court.
This means they know what they've done
is wrong, there's no possible way they
can make it right, and their only hope for
redemption is to ask the court to extend
what they don't deserve: mercy. God extends
mercy to us each day. He's sentenced us
to life—eternal life—and to the freedom
to grow in the shelter of His love.

If I say, "My foot slips," your mercy,
O LORD, will hold me up.
PSALM 94:18 NKJV

There's safety in planting yourself in a
recliner and interacting with the world via
big-screen TV. No real relationships to
let you down or challenge you to grow up.
Nothing to risk, so no chance to fail. But
nowhere in scripture do we see inaction as
God's plan for our lives. We're designed to
live, love, and grow. Along the way, we'll
also fall. It's part of being human. God's
mercy gives us the courage to risk trying
again.

Nature

He determines the number of the
stars and calls them each by name.

PSALM 147:4 NIV

Like a child who carefully chooses the
silver crayon to draw the dog with stars for
eyes, God's artwork is an expression of who
He is. It displays His creativity, attention
to detail, love of diversity, meticulous
organization, and even His sense of humor.
Taking time to contemplate the beauty and
complexity of nature can help paint a clearer
picture for you of what God is like. He's an
artist, as well as a Father, Savior, and friend.

The Lord merely spoke,
and the heavens were created.
He breathed the word,
and all the stars were born.

PSALM 33:6 NLT

Genesis tells us how God spoke nothing into something. But that "something" was not just anything. It was the divine artwork of creation. All of creation, from the tiniest microbe to the most expansive nebula, is wonderful in the fullest sense of the word. Take time to appreciate the wonder God has woven into the world. Take a walk in a park. Fill a vase with fresh flowers. Pet a puppy. Plant a petunia. Then, thank God.

Patience

Be patient and trust the LORD.
Don't let it bother you when all goes
well for those who do sinful things.

PSALM 37:7 CEV

When we encounter conflict or injustice, we want resolution. We want relationships to be mended and wrongs to be made right. We want villains to pay and victims to heal. Now. Wanting this life to resemble heaven is a God-given desire. But the fact is, we're not home yet. If you're impatient for a situation to change, pray for perspective, do what you can, then trust God for resolution in His time and in His way.

My eyes strain to see your rescue,
to see the truth of your
promise fulfilled.

PSALM 119:123 NLT

In an age of microwave meals, instant access, and ATMs, patience is fast becoming a lost virtue. Heaven forbid we're forced to use dial-up instead of broadband! But waiting is part of God's plan. It takes time for babies to mature, for seasons to change, for fruit to ripen, and sometimes for prayers to be answered. Having to wait on God's timing reminds us that God is not our genie in a bottle. He's our sovereign Lord.

Peace

Let them continually say,
"Great is the LORD, who delights in
blessing his servant with peace!"

PSALM 35:27 NLT

The peace God pours out on those who
follow Him runs deeper than peace of mind.
It overflows into peace of heart. As you
trust God a little more each day, placing the
things you cherish most in His loving hands,
you will release a need to control, a tendency
toward worry, and a fear for the future. In
their place, you will discover the comfort of
being cared for like a child being held in a
parent's nurturing embrace.

> Love and faithfulness meet
> together; righteousness and
> peace kiss each other.
>
> PSALM 85:10 NIV

When you follow God's lead and do what you know He wants you to do, you discover a place of peace. Outward struggles may continue, but inside you can relax. You've done what you could with what God has given you—and that's enough. Listen for God's whisper of, "Well done, my beautiful daughter." It's there. Rest in that place of peace and allow yourself to celebrate how far you've come and to anticipate what is still ahead.

Perseverance

Stay with GOD! Take heart. Don't quit.
I'll say it again: Stay with GOD.

PSALM 27:14 MSG

Life is short, but some days seem to last
forever. When you're facing a difficult
day, don't face it alone. Take a good look
at your exhaustion, anxiety, and fears.
Picture entrusting them, one-by-one, into
God's hands. Then take an objective look
at what you need to do today. Invite God to
join you as you take one step at a time in
accomplishing what lies ahead. Throughout
the day, remind yourself that God is right
by your side.

Count yourself lucky,
how happy you must be—
you get a fresh start,
your slate's wiped clean.

PSALM 32:1 MSG

It's hard to keep moving forward if you're dragging along baggage that weighs you down. God wants to help you discard what you don't need. Insecurity, guilt, shame, bad habits, past mistakes—leave them by the side of the road. Jesus has already paid the price for their removal. Once your past is truly behind you, you'll find it much easier to persevere. Tackling only one day at a time is downright doable with God's help.

Power

My power and my strength come from
the LORD, and he has saved me.

PSALM 118:14 CEV

Moses parted the Red Sea. Peter walked
upon the waves. David slaughtered a giant
with a single stone. God's power was the
force behind them all. How will God's power
work through you? Perhaps you'll conquer
an addiction, face your fear of public
speaking, forgive what seems unforgivable,
serve the homeless, or lead someone into
a closer relationship with God. When God
is honored through what you do, you can be
sure His power is at work in you.

Only you are God!
And your power alone,
so great and fearsome,
is worthy of praise.

PSALM 99:3 CEV

God's power is mightier than any
created thing. After all, God simply spoke,
and the power of His words brought
everything else into existence. That kind
of power can move mountains—or change
lives. God's power is at work to help you
accomplish things you never would have
dreamed of doing on your own. Whatever
God leads you to do, He will provide the
power you need to see it through.

Praise

Better is one day in your courts
than a thousand elsewhere.

PSALM 84:10 NIV

What words would you use to describe
God? Loving. Forgiving. Powerful.
Creative. Wise. Merciful. Eternal. Glorious.
Dependable. Truthful. Compassionate.
Faithful. Friend. Father. Savior. Every word
you can think of is reason for praise. When
you pray, share more than a list of requests
with God. Tell God how much He means to
you. Choose one attribute of God and tell
Him how that character trait has made a
difference in your life.

> Sing to the LORD a new song,
> for he has done marvelous things.
>
> PSALM 98:1 NIV

Consider the wide variety of ways we can tell people we love how wonderful they are: send flowers, hire a skywriter, write a poem, proclaim it via Twitter, send a card, share a hug. The list goes on and on. The same is true for the ways we can praise God. We can pray, sing, dance, write our own psalm, use our God-given talents and resources in ways that honor Him. What novel way will you praise God today?

Prayer

I've thrown myself headlong into your
arms—I'm celebrating your rescue.
I'm singing at the top of my lungs,
I'm so full of answered prayers.

PSALM 13:5–6 MSG

When we pray, we expect things to
happen—and they do. Inviting the Creator
of the universe to be intimately involved
in the details of our day is a mysterious
and miraculous undertaking. But prayer
isn't a tool. It's a conversation. God is not
our almighty personal planner, helping
us manage our lives more efficiently.
He's Someone who loves us. When you
pray, remember you're speaking to
Someone who enjoys you, as well as
takes care of you.

God's there, listening for
all who pray, for all who pray
and mean it.

PSALM 145:18 MSG

God is always attentive, listening for
the voice of His children. Like a mother
who hears her child's cry through a baby
monitor in the middle of the night, God
acts on what He hears. He draws near to
comfort, protect, and guide. Never hesitate
to call on Him—anytime, anywhere. He isn't
bothered by your questions or put off by an
overflow of emotion. What touches your life
touches Him.

Presence of God

My soul thirsts for God,
for the living God.
When can I go and meet with God?

PSALM 42:2 NIV

When you're in love, you long to be with the one who has captured your heart. It makes little difference if you're sharing a sumptuous sunset dinner cruise or toiling together to complete a mundane task. What matters is that you're together. When we first get to know God, we long to spend time with Him because of what He provides. But the longer we spend in His presence, the more we desire Him simply because of who He is.

> I cry to God to help me.
> From his palace he hears my call;
> my cry brings me right into his
> presence—a private audience!

PSALM 18:6 MSG

It can be difficult to picture yourself in the presence of Someone you cannot see. But the Bible assures us God is near. His Spirit not only surrounds us, but moves within us. When God's presence feels far away, remember that what you feel is not an accurate gauge of the truth. Read the Psalms to remind yourself that others have felt the way you do. Then, follow the psalmists' example. Continue praising God and moving ahead in faith.

Protection

The angel of the LORD encamps
around those who fear him,
and he delivers them.

PSALM 34:7 NIV

In the Bible we read about angelic beings
who act as God's messengers and warriors.
Far from cute little cherubs who do nothing
more than pluck harps on cotton ball clouds,
we meet angels who yield swords and have
ferocious lionlike faces. But the message
they continually tell God's children is,
"Be not afraid." When you're in need of
protection, remember there's more going
on than is visible to the eye. God's
angels have your back.

> Let all who take refuge in you be glad; let them ever sing for joy. Spread your protection over them, that those who love your name may rejoice in you.

PSALM 5:11 NIV

In the Old Testament, God designates cities of refuge. These were places where people who'd accidentally killed someone could flee. Here they'd be safe from the vengeance of angry relatives until they'd received a fair trial or had proven their innocence. God is a place of refuge for His children. No matter what happens, you're under God's protection. Flee to Him in prayer when you feel under attack. God provides a safe haven where truth will be brought to light.

Provision

Each day that we live,
he provides for our needs and gives
us the strength of a young eagle.

PSALM 103:5 CEV

What do you need today? Whether it's the finances to pay a fast-approaching bill or the courage to have a difficult conversation with a friend, God wants to provide what you need. Share your heart with Him. But before you rush off to other things, sit quietly and listen. God may reveal how you can work with Him to meet that need. He may also want to help you share with others what He's already so generously provided.

He covers the heavens with clouds,
provides rain for the earth,
and makes the grass grow
in mountain pastures.

PSALM 147:8 NLT

God provides for us in so many ways
that it's easy to take them for granted.
The fact that the sun rises each morning,
encouraging crops to grow, or that our heart
takes its next beat and our lungs their next
breath are just a few of the countless gifts
we receive from God's almighty hand. As
you go through the day, consider the big and
little ways God meets your needs. Then take
time at day's end to give thanks.

Purpose

I cry out to God Most High, to God,
who fulfills his purpose for me.

PSALM 57:2 NIV

A beautiful woman like yourself was created for more than decoration. You were created for a purpose. Your purpose is not a specific job God has designated for you to accomplish. It's more like a unique spot He's designed for you to fill. God is working with you, encouraging you to grow into this "sweet spot." As you learn to lean on Him, God will help you discover the true joy and significance that come from simply being "you."

> God's plan for the world
> stands up, all his designs
> are made to last.
>
> PSALM 33:11 MSG

In Exodus we read how God asked
Moses to lead the children of Israel
out of slavery in Egypt. Moses said yes to
the leading but no to the public speaking.
Moses' "no" didn't prevent God's plan
from taking place. God used Aaron, Moses'
brother, to be His spokesperson in Moses'
stead. God's purpose and plan for this world
will happen. God has given you the free will
to say whether you'll take part or not. What
will your answer be?

Relationships

Keep company with God,
get in on the best.

PSALM 37:4 MSG

Sometimes, drawing close to God can feel like an eternal to-do list instead of a relationship. If praying, reading scripture, going to church, or serving others begins to feel like just another task, don't settle for checking them off your list. That's ritual, not relationship. Instead, make a date with God. Set up a time and place. Then simply talk and listen. Focus on who God is.

Take the time to fall in love with Him all over again.

I pray that the LORD will let your family and your descendants always grow strong.

PSALM 115:14 CEV

Praying for the people you care about is one way of loving them. When you pray for them, you invite God to work in their lives. What more loving gift could there be than that? But prayer also softens your own heart toward those you're praying for. With God's help, you feel their needs more deeply, understand their motivations more clearly, and can forgive their faults more completely. There's no downside to lifting those you love up in prayer.

Renewal

*Weeping may remain for a night,
but rejoicing comes in the morning.*

PSALM 30:5 NIV

Renewal isn't taking a deep breath, smiling through gritted teeth, and muscling your way through today. Renewal is a kind of rebirth. It's letting the past fall from your shoulders and welcoming hope back into your heart. Renewal is a work of the Spirit, not a state of mind or act of the will. It's joining hands with God and moving forward together, expectant and refreshed. Are you ready to release whatever's holding you back and reach out to God?

> Create in me a clean heart,
> O God, and renew a
> steadfast spirit within me.
>
> PSALM 51:10 NKJV

Laundry is an ongoing process. You wear clothes, soil them, and then wash them over and over again. But even after washing, clothes are never really new again. Don't confuse God's forgiveness with a trip to the Laundromat. When God forgives you, He doesn't just wash away your sins, He gives you a totally clean heart. There's no dull residue or faint stains of rebellion. You're renewed—not reused or recycled or "just like new." Your heart's new. Again.

Respect

But I, by your great mercy,
will come into your house;
in reverence will I bow down
toward your holy temple.

PSALM 5:7 NIV

It's true God is our Friend. But He's more
than our BFF (Best Friend Forever). God
is our sovereign Lord and King. He's the
One who initiated this implausibly intimate
relationship, Creator with creation. But
God's overwhelming love for us should not
lull us into a familiarity that disregards
reverence and respect. There will come a
time when every knee will bow to Him.
Until that day, may our awe and esteem
continue to grow right along with
our love.

Come, my children, listen as
I teach you to respect the LORD.

PSALM 34:11 CEV

Consider the teachers and leaders that have helped draw you closer to God. These people are worthy of your thanks and prayers, but they're also worthy of your respect. The Bible tells us God is the power behind those in authority. But these people are still human. They make mistakes. They make decisions we don't always agree with. We aren't asked to blindly follow, but we are asked to love. Respect is one side of that love.

Rest

He makes me lie down in green
pastures, he leads me beside quiet
waters, he restores my soul.

PSALM 23:2–3 NIV

God created the world in six days. Then
He took a day to sit back and enjoy all of the
good things He'd done. The Bible tells us
God doesn't tire or sleep, but even He knew
the value of a time-out. If you're weary,
or simply trying to keep up with a hectic
schedule, let God lead you beside quiet
waters. Look back over what you and God
have accomplished together. Rejoice, then
rest so God can restore.

> He who dwells in the shelter
> of the Most High will rest in
> the shadow of the Almighty.

PSALM 91:1 NIV

Picture a hammock in the shade of two leafy trees, swaying gently in the breeze. Now picture yourself nestled there, eyes closed, totally relaxed. This is what it's like to rest in the shadow of the Almighty. Knowing that God holds you tenderly in His hand, offering protection, comfort, and grace, allows you to let go of your fears and concerns. God knows about them all. Rest in the fact that scripture says nothing is impossible with God.

Reward

By your teachings, Lord,
I am warned; by obeying them,
I am greatly rewarded.

PSALM 19:11 CEV

Doing the right thing comes with its
own rewards. Whether it's the actual Ten
Commandments or other teachings found
in scripture, following what God says is right
points the way toward loving relationships
and a balanced life. Obedience comes with
the added bonus of a guilt-free conscience
and the knowledge that we're living a life
that pleases the Father who so deeply
loves us. These are rewards that won't
tarnish with the passing of time.

You, O Lord, are loving.
Surely you will reward each person
according to what he has done.

PSALM 62:12 NIV

Revelation, the final book of the Bible, gives us a peek at what heaven will be like. One thing we discover is that we'll be rewarded for what we've done here on earth. But instead of putting these rewards on display in our heavenly mansions, we're told that the elders in the group will lay these rewards before God's throne. That's truly where they belong. God is the one who enables and inspires us to do what's worth rewarding.

Righteousness

Your righteousness is like the
mighty mountains, your justice
like the ocean depths. You care for
people and animals alike, O Lord.

PSALM 36:6 NLT

God's goodness is more than Him playing
"nice." God's goodness is an extension of
His righteousness. Since God is loving and
just, the morally virtuous thing for Him to
do is provide His children with a balance of
mercy and discipline, guidelines and grace.
That's why a price had to be paid for our
sins. God's righteousness demanded it. But
God's love allowed Jesus to pay a debt we
couldn't afford to pay on our own.

164

Blessed are those who
keep justice, and he who does
righteousness at all times!

PSALM 106:3 NKJV

Living a moral life, a life that
honors God and those around you, is
righteousness in action. It's the opposite
of self-righteousness. That's a life where
you justify doing what you deem right,
regardless of whether God agrees with
your assessment. Righteousness, however,
reflects God's own character. It shows
you truly are His child. Your actions are
not swayed by emotion, peer pressure, or
personal gain. You do what's right
simply because it's the right
thing to do.

Sacrifice

The sacrifices of God are a broken spirit; a broken and contrite heart, O God, you will not despise.

PSALM 51:17 NIV

Sacrifice can be motivated by love, necessity, or obligation. God asks only for sacrifices motivated by our love for Him. That doesn't mean they don't come at a price. When we place our own pride on the altar and acknowledge that God is in control and we are not, it can be painful. But it's like the pain that follows a much-needed surgery. It's a precursor to healing. What we give up out of love, we're better off without.

I am God Most High! The only
sacrifice I want is for you to be
thankful and to keep your word.

PSALM 50:14 CEV

In the Old Testament, we read about God's
people offering sacrifices to pay the price
for their rebellion against God. In the New
Testament, these sacrifices disappear—
except one. When Jesus willingly went to
the cross for us, He became the ultimate
sacrifice. His death paid for the wrongs
we've done once and for all. Each time we
choose to follow God instead of our own
hearts, we offer a sacrifice of thanks in
return for all Jesus has done.

Satisfaction

Satisfy us each morning with your
unfailing love, so we may sing
for joy to the end of our lives.

PSALM 90:14 NLT

Each morning when you rise, take time
to turn your eyes toward the Son. Take a
fresh look at what Jesus has done out of love
for you. Recall what you've been forgiven
and the many blessings you've received.
Consider how following in Jesus' footsteps
has changed the direction of your life—and
will change the day ahead. Allow gratitude
to wash over you anew. There's no greater
satisfaction than seeing your life in the
light of God's great love.

> You open your hand
> and satisfy the desires
> of every living thing.
>
> PSALM 145:16 NIV

Our hearts are needy. They cry out for love, relief, pleasure, and purpose. They cry out for what they see on TV. Only God can quiet their relentless cry. That's because God is what they're actually crying out for. As we open our hearts more fully to God, we'll see more clearly that our needs are being met. What's more, we'll notice that our desires are changing, aligning themselves more and more with God's own.

Security

The LORD is truthful;
he can be trusted.

PSALM 33:4 CEV

God's power is limitless. That's tough to comprehend. But knowing God has the ability to care for us in any and all circumstances is not the true reason why we can feel safe and secure in His presence. Being in the presence of a beefy bodyguard only feels safe if you know that person is trustworthy, if you know he's on your side. God is on your side, fighting for you. You can trust His strength and His love.

> You are my hiding place;
> you will protect me from
> trouble and surround me
> with songs of deliverance.
>
> PSALM 32:7 NIV

Having an alarm system installed in your home can give you a sense of security. If someone tries to break in, you can trust that help is immediately on the way. God is a 24-hour security system. When you call, He's there. But the truth is, God's there even before you call. He won't hesitate to step in to protect you, even if you're unaware of the danger you're in.

Serving God

Make my heart glad!
I serve you, and my prayer is sincere.
PSALM 86:4 CEV

The people we love, we serve. If a friend's car breaks down, we give her a lift. If she's ill, we make her family a meal. We may use the word *help* instead of *serve*, but the result is the same. Love leads us to act. As our love for God grows, so will our desire to serve Him. One way we serve God is to care for those He loves. Ask God whom He'd like you to serve today.

> Serve the LORD with gladness;
> Come before His presence
> with singing.
>
> PSALM 100:2 NKJV

We live in a needy world. People around the globe need food and medical care. People in our city need shelter. Our church needs volunteers to serve in the nursery. We can't fill every need. And God doesn't expect us to. We have limited time, energy, and resources. That's why prayer is such an important part of serving. Only with God's help will we have the wisdom and courage to say yes or no to the opportunities that surround us.

Sleep

*I think about you before I go to sleep,
and my thoughts turn to
you during the night.*

PSALM 63:6 CEV

Close your day in a wonderful way by
spending it in your Father's arms. Instead
of allowing your thoughts to race ahead
toward tomorrow, take time to savor today.
Regardless of whether it's been a day
you'll long remember or one you'd rather
forget, ask God to help you recall what
matters. Thank Him for His loving care. Ask
forgiveness for any moments when you
turned your back on Him. Then relax
and rest, knowing He's near.

You've kept track of my every toss
and turn through the sleepless nights,
each tear entered in your ledger,
each ache written in your book.

PSALM 56:8 MSG

Insomnia can feel like a curse. Your mind races and your body aches for rest. When sleep is elusive, rest in God. Set your mind on Him, instead of on what lies heavy on your heart. Meditate on a single verse of scripture, allowing the truth of God's words to release the tension from your body and the muddle in your mind. Curl up in the crook of God's arm and let Him draw you toward dreams worth dreaming.

Speech

May the words of my mouth
and the meditation of my heart
be pleasing in your sight,
O LORD, my Rock and my Redeemer.

PSALM 19:14 NIV

God hears the words you speak. He even hears the ones that remain unsaid anywhere other than your mind. Sometimes it's hard to get words past your lips. It's difficult to apologize, comfort someone who's hurting, or try to untangle miscommunication in a relationship. It can even be difficult to say, "I love you." With God's help, you can say what needs to be said. Ask God to help you speak the right words at the right time.

> Set a guard over my mouth,
> O Lord; keep watch over
> the door of my lips.
>
> PSALM 141:3 NIV

The words we speak have power. They can hurt or heal, repel or attract. They also provide a fairly accurate barometer as to what's going on in our hearts. If you find words slipping out that you wish you could take back, return to the source. Ask God to reveal what's going on in your heart. With God's help, your words can become a welcome source of comfort and encouragement to those around you.

Spiritual Growth

Be still, and know that I am God.
PSALM 46:10 NIV

What season of spiritual growth are you in? Springtime's early bud of new love? Basking in summer's sunshine, growing by fruitful leaps and bounds? Knee-deep in autumn, with remnants of your old life falling like dead leaves around your feet? Or praying your way through winter, where God and that joy of first love seem far away? Whatever season you're in, remember: God's the only One who can make something grow. Trust His timing and watch for fruit.

> Blessed are those whose strength
> is in you, who have set their
> hearts on pilgrimage.
>
> PSALM 84:5 NIV

You're embarking on a lifelong spiritual journey. It's a pilgrimage that will follow a different path than that of anyone else who has ever desired to grow closer to God. The prayers you pray, how quickly you mature, the battles you fight, the challenges you overcome, and the person you become will all add up to a one-of-a-kind adventure. Look to God instead of comparing yourself to others to gauge how far you've come and what direction you're headed next.

Starting Over

GOD made my life complete when
I placed all the pieces before him.
When I got my act together,
he gave me a fresh start.

PSALM 18:20 MSG

Picture your life as a jigsaw puzzle. You've been trying to put it together for years, with limited success. Some pieces are lost or bent beyond recognition. What's worse is that you have no idea what the final picture is supposed to be. Want a do-over? God offers you one. Simply admit you need His help. Then hand the pieces of your life over to Him. God will help you create a life that's beautiful, significant, and complete.

> I feel put back together,
> and I'm watching my step.
> GOD rewrote the text of my
> life when I opened the book
> of my heart to his eyes.
>
> PSALM 18:24 MSG

God can rewrite your life's story line.
It's true that what's done is done—God
won't change the past—but He can change
how you see it. He can reveal how He has
woven themes of redemption and blessing
throughout what once looked hopeless. He
can also change how the past affects you.
Through His power, God can free you from
the bondage of bad habits and past mistakes.
As for the future, that's a fresh page. What
will God and you cowrite?

Strength

Pile your troubles on God's
shoulders—he'll carry your load,
he'll help you out.

PSALM 55:22 MSG

You can gain physical strength by heading
to the gym. However, spiritual strength is
what you need to carry you through life.
Instead of lifting weights, lift your eyes
and prayers toward heaven. Stretch your
compassion by reaching out to those around
you in love. Get your heart pumping as you
push beyond your own limitations and rely
more completely on God. Through it all,
God will be your strength as well as your
personal trainer.

O my Strength, I watch for you;
you, O God, are my fortress,
my loving God.

PSALM 59:9–10 NIV

Some people believe that if they follow God, life will be trouble-free. Jesus doesn't seem to agree. In John 16:33 (NIV), Jesus says, "In this world you will have trouble." But Jesus doesn't leave it at that. He continues, "But take heart! I have overcome the world." Don't be surprised when struggle comes, but don't lose heart either. God will provide the strength you need when you need it to help you overcome whatever comes your way.

Success

*May he grant your heart's desires
and make all your plans succeed.*

PSALM 20:4 NLT

It's tempting to do what we want—while asking God to bless what we do. But a "please bless my efforts" prayer is not a rubber stamp of God's approval or our success. Regardless of what's on your agenda today, invite God to be part of your plans—from the conception stage right through to the celebration of its completion. God will help you align your motives and methods with His own and succeed in the ways that matter most.

> They are like trees growing
> beside a stream, trees that
> produce fruit in season and
> always have leaves. Those people
> succeed in everything they do.

PSALM 1:3 CEV

How do you measure success? By your title? Your weight? Your net worth? The opinion of others? God's measure of success has little to do with accolades, appearance, acquisitions, or admiration. According to the Bible, the key to real success is love. The more we love God and others, the more successful we are at fulfilling what God has planned for our lives. Want to be a truly successful woman? Serve others with a humble heart.

Thankfulness

What a beautiful thing, GOD, to give
thanks, to sing an anthem to you, the
High God! To announce your love
each daybreak, sing your faithful
presence all through the night.

PSALM 92:1 MSG

It used to be considered proper etiquette to
send a handwritten thank-you note for every
gift you received. Consider how high a stack
of note cards you'd need if you formally
thanked God for every gift He's given.
Sending a thank-you via prayer or singing
God's praises are the most common ways
God's children express their gratitude to
Him. But don't let that stop you from
getting creative. What new way can
you thank God today?

Now I'm alert to GOD's ways;
I don't take God for granted.

PSALM 18:21 MSG

The phrase "Thank God!" has lost much of its meaning these days. People use it interchangeably with expressions such as, "Wow!" "Thank goodness!" or "I really lucked out!" That's because people feel a surge of gratitude when good things happen to them, but not all of them are certain where they should direct their thanks. You've caught a glimpse of God's goodness. You know who is behind the blessings you receive. Don't hesitate to say, "Thank God!" and mean it.

Thoughts

You have tested my thoughts
and examined my heart in the night.
You have scrutinized me
and found nothing wrong.

PSALM 17:3 NLT

When your mind wanders, where does it go? In your most unguarded moments, when you're no longer focused on deadlines and demands, what you think about is a strong indicator of what matters most to you. Pay attention to where your train of thought leads. Is it a direction you really want to go? If you find your mind traveling roads that draw you away from God, set your thoughts back on track toward what's truly worth focusing on.

> I try to count your thoughts,
> but they outnumber the grains
> of sand on the beach. And when
> I awake, I will find you nearby.
>
> PSALM 139:18 CEV

Trying to comprehend an infinite God with a finite brain can leave you feeling small. That's okay. Compared to God, we are. But when we balance the fact that a God too big for our brains to hold cares for us with a love so deep that nothing, absolutely nothing, can come between us, we find peace, as well as perspective. Turn your thoughts toward God, and your heart can't help but follow.

Trust

Some trust in chariots and some in horses, but we trust in the name of the Lord our God.

PSALM 20:7 NIV

In the United States our currency proclaims, "In God We Trust." That's easier said than done. It can be tempting to trust more in the money this motto is printed on than in God Himself. That's because trusting God means trusting someone we cannot see. It's like trusting an invisible chair to hold your weight. You may believe it's there, but actually sitting down takes faith. When your trust wavers, recall God's faithfulness to you. Then step out in faith—and sit.

Far better to take refuge in GOD
than trust in people; far better to
take refuge in GOD than trust
in celebrities.

PSALM 118:8–9 MSG

Trust is a gift. If we're wise, we extend
it to those who are worthy of receiving it.
Witnessing character traits such as honesty,
integrity, loyalty, and love in a person's
life lets us know that our trust hasn't been
misplaced. But even trustworthy people let
us down on occasion. The same cannot be
said of God. God never falters or fails. He is
eternally trustworthy. What do you need to
trust God for today?

Truth

Unspoken truth is spoken everywhere.

PSALM 19:4 MSG

God's truth is made known through the Bible. But it's also proclaimed throughout all of His creation. The seasons speak of God's faithfulness. The night sky sings of His glory. Thunderstorms shout of His might. And the first heartbeat of each child whispers, "Yes, God still performs miracles." Listen for God's truth as you go through your day. Take what you hear and compare it with what you read in God's Word. God's truth isn't concealed. It's revealed every day.

What you're after is truth from the inside out. Enter me, then; conceive a new, true life.

PSALM 51:6 MSG

God knows the truth about you—and He wants you to know it, too. He wants you to put away the lies you've been listening to, the ones that whisper, "I'm not enough—smart enough, pretty enough, young enough, successful enough, loved enough, good enough." Whatever "not enough" you struggle with, ask God to help you see the truth. Then dare to go a step further by not only accepting the truth about yourself but living your life in light of it.

Waiting

My soul waits for the LORD more than watchmen wait for the morning, more than watchmen wait for the morning.

PSALM 130:6 NIV

Waiting may seem like a passive pursuit. However, you actually have a choice as to how you'll spend your time. You can waste it, worry over it, or worship through it. It doesn't matter what you're waiting for—an overdue flight, the results of a medical test, an answer to prayer—choosing to worship turns waiting into watching. The more often you turn your eyes toward God, the better chance you'll have of noticing how His hand is in the details.

God, the one and only— I'll wait
as long as he says. Everything I hope
for comes from him, so why not?

PSALM 62:5 MSG

Sometimes God's timing feels out of sync
with our own. Considering 2 Peter 3:8 (NIV)
tells us that "with the Lord a day is like
a thousand years, and a thousand years
are like a day," it's no wonder. God is on
an eternal time schedule. Ours is more
temporal. But God sees the big picture,
which we cannot. That's why waiting on His
timing is a wise thing to do.

Wholeness

Keep your eye on the healthy soul,
scrutinize the straight life; there's
a future in strenuous wholeness.

PSALM 37:37 MSG

The word *holistic* is often linked with medicine. It describes an approach to treatment that addresses the whole person instead of just the physical symptoms. If you read the Gospels, you'll see this is how Jesus cared for people. He met their physical, mental, and emotional needs as well as their spiritual ones. It's not only your eternity that matters to God; it's your here and now.

Invite God into every corner of your life. He cares about them all.

> GOD will help me. At dusk,
> dawn, and noon I sigh deep
> sighs—he hears, he rescues.
> My life is well and whole, secure
> in the middle of danger.
>
> PSALM 55:16–17 MSG

You may think you're living a balanced life. You eat right, exercise regularly, and try to limit stress by allowing breathing room in your schedule. But if you're not taking care of your spiritual needs, your life is still out of balance. It's like trying to take a solo seesaw ride. It can't be done. Welcoming God into the ups and downs of each day is the key to wholeness. Is God's peace the missing piece in your life?

Wisdom

Our days are numbered. That isn't a warning. It's a promise. Nothing can cut our lives short of what God has ordained for each one of us to live. Living life in light of our mortality isn't a morose pastime. It's a mind-set that can help us make wise choices. We have a limited time to live and love on earth. Being more intentional about how we spend our time is one simple way to help make each day count.

If you are really wise,
you'll think this over—it's time you
appreciated GOD's deep love.
PSALM 107:42 MSG

Without wisdom, knowledge is just a bunch of information. Who cares if you have all the answers but are clueless when it comes to applying what you know? If you want to be a wise woman, the Bible says all you need to do is ask. God will impart to you understanding and insight that goes beyond your own personal experience. Once you understand the wise thing to do, all that remains is doing it.

Wonder

Far and wide they'll come to a stop,
they'll stare in awe, in wonder.
Dawn and dusk take turns calling,
"Come and worship."

PSALM 65:8 MSG

Children are known for their sense of
wonder. Maybe that's because there's so
much they don't know. The closer we draw
to God, the more we realize how much we
are like children—how much we really don't
know. When you focus on God, take time
to give yourself over to childlike wonder.
That's worship in its purest and most
spontaneous form. You don't need to know
all the answers, as long as you know
the One behind them all.

People use the word *awesome* to describe everything from landing a difficult snowboarding maneuver to evaluating a pair of Jimmy Choo shoes. But at the heart of the word lies its original intent: declaring something worthy of our awe. When it comes to inspiring awe, nothing can compare to God. Everything He does and everything He is, is totally awesome. Really. Allow the truth of what you know about God to really sink in. Wonder—and awe—is certain to follow.

Work

Unless the LORD builds the house,
its builders labor in vain.
Unless the LORD watches over the city,
the watchmen stand guard in vain.

PSALM 127:1 NIV

Working hard without God is simply hard work. Working hard with God's help can be part of a great enterprise. When you honor God with what you do—by turning to Him with your decisions, treating coworkers as people God dearly loves, and doing your job as if God were your boss—your time on the job is transformed into a time of worship.

Your job title isn't as significant as your willingness to let God work through you.

You will eat the fruit of your labor; blessings and prosperity will be yours.

PSALM 128:2 NIV

Some blessings are ours simply because God loves us. Other blessings come as a result of working with God. When it's within our ability, God expects us to play an active role in answering our own prayers. We pray for provision yet continue to perform faithfully at work. We pray for better marriages yet do our part to love and forgive. We pray for better health yet watch what we eat. Between our labor and God's love, we're doubly blessed.

Worry

The fear of bad news is what worry is all about. Trusting God is what makes that fear fade away. So the next time fear begins tugging at your heart, turn every worry that's weighing you down into a prayer. The more this becomes habit, the more you'll notice your perspective beginning to change. You'll start to anticipate seeing God bring something good out of any and every situation. For God, even bad news is an opportunity to work miracles.

Search me, O God,
and know my heart;
test me and know my
anxious thoughts.

PSALM 139:23 NIV

Women have a reputation as worriers. But that's not a reputation God wants you to reinforce. God offers peace in place of worry and anxiety. Who wouldn't want to accept a trade like that? When your anxious thoughts start steamrolling their way through your mind, treat yourself like a toddler. Put yourself in a time-out. Close your eyes, breathe deep, and give God your worries one by one. Allow God to quiet your mind and your heart.

Worship

Blessed are you who give
yourselves over to GOD,
turn your backs on the world's
"sure thing," ignore what
the world worships.

PSALM 40:4 MSG

What do you worship, really? Approval,
financial security, youth, talent—even food—
can be idols that seem to promise a happier,
more satisfying life. But it's a promise that
nothing and no one can keep except God.
Having the picture-perfect summer home or
snacking on the world's richest cheesecake
can make you feel good for a while. But
they possess no real power—or answers
to anything that truly matters. Only
God is worthy of our worship and
our love.

On your feet now—applaud GOD!
Bring a gift of laughter, sing
yourselves into his presence.

PSALM 100:1 MSG

Sunday mornings at church are often referred to as a "worship service." But worship isn't a service or duty. It's a response. It's your personal reply to God's goodness, power, majesty, and love. If worship isn't how you react when you draw near to God, perhaps you need to draw closer. Read the Psalms aloud. Pray with your arms outstretched and your face flat on the floor. Get alone with the Creator of the universe and let your worship flow.

Scripture Index

Notes

Notes

Notes

Notes

Notes

Notes

Notes

Notes